Altered before the Altar:

Devotional Study Guide

Erica D. Hearns

ALTERED BEFORE THE ALTAR: DEVOTIONAL STUDY GUIDE

Serious Season Press

©2014 by Erica D. Hearns

ISBN 13: 978-0990743019

Cover Image & Design by Erica D. Hearns, Serious Season Press

For information regarding special discounts for bulk purchase, please contact Serious Season Press at inquiries@aseriousseason.com

Dedicated in loving memory of Keith Leon Taylor, Sr. Your steadfast belief in me and pride in the woman I was becoming will remain with me for always.

Contents

Acknowledgments

Sometimes God provides us with answers to the questions we have in unexpected ways. I thought that I was finished with the topic of preparing for marriage when I published *Altered before the Altar,* but I couldn't stop thinking of all the activities and discussions I had to trim from the final version. God kept pressing those things, and many more, on my heart, and I am forever grateful that He again trusted me to share with in helping single women become more focused on and dedicated to Him. Thank you, Father, for pushing me to go deeper and do more when I *really* didn't think I had any more to give (and between me and you, any more to learn. How silly was I?).

This time around, I must thank my critique partners, Christina Yother and Dana R. Lynn for talking me off the ledge when I went out on it during this wild ride. You ladies are fabulous writers and I love reading your work before anyone else gets to. Thank you both for all of your support and encouragement throughout this journey.

Thank you to my church family at the Westmoreland Drive Church of Christ. All of you have blessed me so much the last seven years. I know that I am a better Christian and person from having been able to labor together with you. Thank you for your support of me and *Altered*, from conceding to interviews and reading rough drafts, to those who continually asked about my progress and encouraged me to finish. Thank you for your gentle and not so gentle rebukes and corrections, and the many ways in which you have pushed me to grow out of my comfort zone.

I owe a special debt of gratitude to Dr. Gerri Tartt, who gave me the idea for the Naked Challenge and the Naked Devotionals during her workshop on purity a few years ago. I greatly admire the woman that you are and how much you give back to those around you. I hope to be like you when I grow up!

I'm endlessly thankful to everyone who has supported *Altered before the Altar* thus far. Your encouragement and praise have meant a great deal to me. It still feels odd when you tell me how much you enjoyed the book or how it was just what you needed, but as long as God is glorified in it, I'll suffer through. ☺

Lastly, but by no means least, I would be remiss if I didn't mention my younger brothers, Keith Leon Taylor, Jr. and Obed Hearns. Being a big sister to you two has blessed me beyond measure. I've learned so much trying to teach you. I hope you both know how much your "little big sister" loves you.

Author's Note

Whenever an author finishes a book, there's a great sense of satisfaction accompanied by a nagging feeling that there's still something more to be said, or a better way to have phrased something. I suppose this is especially true when it comes to a book like *Altered before the Altar*.

The main goal that I had for *Altered before the Altar* was that it not only be filled with sound biblical principles but that it would provide practical information that women could apply to their lives no matter what season of life they were in. I wanted *Altered* to encourage single Christian women to strive to better themselves and their relationship with God, and to use the principles and instructions found in His word to make the best decisions for their romantic future. More than just giving women something to think about, I wanted to give them something to *do*. I'd like to think that I made a convincing case for following God's lead on love & marriage, but I wasn't as sure that I'd provided enough tools for women to think critically about these areas beyond what was written.

When I pressed publish on *Altered before the Altar,* I knew there were still things I wanted the reader to know. I wanted to provide them with questions to guide further discussion and exercises that would help to illustrate certain points I'd made. I wanted to provide devotions that made the personal application of the principles easier. It was at that time I decided to write a companion study guide to *Altered before the Altar*.

The only way to change a habit is to develop a new habit. As Christians, we always have the spirit of God in us that both gives us the desire to be better and helps us to attain better (Phil. 2:13). Yet, as Paul says, when we want to do right, evil is present with us (Rom. 7:21). It is up to us to train and strengthen our discernment through exercising those senses and making our use of them habitual (Heb. 5:14).

Let me be clear: God is the one who changes us for the better. None of the exercises, activities, or devotions in this book by themselves are going to change your life for you. Neither your determination not to be a certain type of person nor your resolve not to do certain things will prevent you from stumbling or falling back into old habits. God changes hearts and minds on a permanent basis. It was the work that God did during baptism that cleansed us, and not our willingness to be baptized. God requires that we come to Him and confess our sins, because only He can forgive our sins and cleanse us from unrighteousness (1 John 1:9).

In this study guide and devotional, then, I'm not trying to help you to save yourself or "get yourself right." I happen to think that *Altered before the Altar* is a good book, but it won't save your soul or change your nature, and neither will this devotional. All any Christian seeks to do is to be a light that shows the glory of God to others so that they may want to know God for themselves.

So consider this study guide a match that I hope will kindle your understanding of the key concepts and principles espoused in *Altered before the Altar*. It is my hope that the original text and the discussions and exercises in this book will help you see your life in relation to God more clearly. It is God's word that will grow you (I Pet. 2:2) and prepare you to consume strong meat (Heb. 5:14). I only hope that I can point you to scriptures that you can feast upon and use to fuel you on your journey.

I pray that the questions, activities and devotions found within these pages will increase your understanding and inspire you to get closer to Christ and deeper into God's word.

I would love to hear your thoughts on *Altered* and this guide. You can leave a comment on the official site of *Altered before the Altar,* www.alteredbeforethealtar.com. You can also email me at mz.zeyzey2@gmail.com, tweet me at @2blu2btru, or follow my Instagram mz_zeyzey2. You can leave reviews for my books on Goodreads and Amazon as well.

XOXO,

Erica D. Hearns

Adam Meet Eve

Nearly every topic addressed throughout *Altered before the Altar* is introduced and discussed in the chapter "Adam, Meet Eve." The "golden points" from this chapter are:

1. Adam had both purpose and provisions before he was given Eve.
2. Adam rests and allows God to provide him with the perfect mate.
3. God gave Eve to Adam
4. God created Eve to fulfill a specific purpose in Adam's life.
5. Adam and Eve were naked and not ashamed.

Discussion Questions

Why is it important that a man have a purpose/job before seeking a mate?

_____

_____

_____

_____

Discuss a time when the job you were doing was not your job.

_____

_____

_____

_____

What are some signs that indicate a person is "asleep" with regard to romantic relationships? Awake? Which are you?

_____

_____

_____

_____

_____

_____

Are you prepared to be presented? Explain.

_____

_____

_____

Would an "Adam" recognize you? Explain.

_____

_____

_____

Which attitude problem describes your attitude toward God? Provide three ways you can change your attitude.

_____

_____

_____

_____

Relate a time when you were guilty of "eating the fruit" (i.e., attempted to better God's plan). Why did you do it? What was the result?

_____

_____

ACTIVITY:

Naked Challenge

We are at our most vulnerable when we are naked. Without anything to protect ourselves or hide behind, we are incapable of concealing any weaknesses in ourselves. Many women struggle with the concept of nakedness not just from a spiritual or emotional standpoint, but from a physical standpoint as well.

For this activity, you MUST stand in the mirror naked each morning for thirty (30) days and identify at least one thing that you like about yourself. You must identify something new each morning—no repetitions. At least 2/3 of these things (20) must be physical attributes.

Write down your selections in your journal, along with an empowering scripture, saying or song, and one thing you are grateful for. You don't have to elaborate if you don't want to-- a simple sentence will do. You can be grateful for the same thing each day, but try to dig deeper and find something new each morning.

The most important goal of this challenge is to shift your focus from the negative to the positive. So often we zero in on what we see as imperfections. Use this exercise as an opportunity to find the beauty in yourself.

Note: If this challenge brings up any feelings best handled by a mental health professional, minister, spiritual counselor, or a medical professional, please seek the assistance of a person qualified in these fields.

NAKED DEVOTIONAL:

"But" Naked

> **12** And the man said, The woman whom thou gavest to be
> with me, she gave me of the tree, and I did eat.

Since the beginning of human existence, people have tried to come up with excuses to relieve themselves of responsibility. Even Adam tried to excuse his sin. When God called him to account for the sin he had committed, Adam blamed Eve. Worse, he also puts the blame on God, since God is the one who gave Eve to Adam. Even though Adam attempts to shift the blame from himself onto Eve, God still punishes him for his disobedience, just as God will punish us for any sin we haven't repented of when we stand before Him in the judgment.

There's a famous quote regarding excuses that I learned in college which states that excuses are the tools of the incompetent. We use excuses when we can't use the truth. Excuses are poor substitutes that build unstable structures on sinking sand. Like the master in the Parable of the Talents, God will not tolerate any of our excuses (Matt 25:14-30). It would be beneficial to us, then, to learn to exist without them today.

Think about your "fall back excuses"-- those excuses you find yourself making regularly to justify your shortcomings. Write them down. Now, examine each one and find a way to overcome this crutch. For example, instead of saying you don't have time to read the Bible, decide to get up ½ an hour earlier or buy an audio version to listen to while in transit. Don't hold on to any excuses. Your soul could be at stake.

DEVOTIONAL:

Naked and Not Ashamed

¹²For the word of God is quick, and powerful, and sharper than any two-edged sword, piercing even to the dividing asunder of soul and spirit, and of the joints and marrow, and is a discerner of the thoughts and intents of the heart.¹³Neither is there any creature that is not manifest in his sight; but all things *are* naked and opened unto the eyes of him with whom we have to do. Heb. 4:12-13

The story of creation ends with the beautiful picture of Adam and Eve, "naked and unashamed." Most biblical commentaries point out how this shows sexuality can be freely expressed within the institution of marriage. But also of note is their spiritual nakedness. Adam and Eve were naked before the Lord and not concerned about how exposed they were to God.

After the Fall, when Adam and Eve heard God, they hid themselves because they were naked. Yet at this time, they weren't *physically* naked; they had sewn fig leaves together to hide their nakedness from one another. It is evident that they felt this outward covering that kept their nakedness hidden from each other was inadequate when it came to hiding from God.

Once their eyes were opened, Adam and Eve began to associate their nakedness with something to be ashamed of, to be hidden. They couldn't be exposed and vulnerable before God anymore; they were afraid of Him.

Many of us stand in the mirror before going out each day and zero in on every little imperfection. We choose clothing or use makeup to camouflage or conceal anything we don't want to show the world and draw attention to the features we want people to notice. We may hide our insecurities behind a know-it-all attitude or over-emphasize our strengths.

This hunt for imperfection can creep into many aspects of our lives, until we are always finding fault with ourselves and become stagnated. We begin to hide things we're ashamed of instead of dealing with them. It's almost as if we get enjoyment out of taking our insecurities out and sighing over them. We wonder why things don't change, when deep down we know that we to weighed down by the things we are trying to conceal to make any progress.

Nakedness makes you vulnerable. There's something about being naked and not having anything to hide behind that highlights and underlines the feelings of guilt and shame associated with how we perceive ourselves. But being completely exposed can allow us to be cleansed. When we confess our sins to God, He is able to wipe away every bit of the residue of defilement we have on us (1 John 1:9). He makes it possible for us to get the grime of shame off of our skin.

God sees who we really are behind all the artifice. His word is the mirror through which we truly see ourselves and how much we really need Him. That is why His word cuts so deeply. God doesn't want us to cover up our failings and frailties; He seeks to remove them. Today, take your shortcomings to God. Pour out those things you are struggling to conceal from the world, the things that no one else sees. Then make time to meditate on God's word concerning those areas.

Single & Satisfied?

In this chapter, contentment, discontentment, and being the bride of Christ are discussed in detail. Contentment is accepting your lot in life without complaint. Contentment says that we know it was God that gave us what we have, and that we trust Him to provide us with anything that we lack. While we should continue to strive to better ourselves and our situations, we must be content with where we are.

The opposite of contentment is discontentment. There are three main causes of discontentment discussed: worry, comparison and covetousness, and boredom/complacency. Worry makes the things that we don't have or what could happen bigger or more important than the things we do have and the trust we have that God will provide. Comparing ourselves to others may cause us to feel as if what we have isn't good enough, and we may even begin to covet the things that another person has acquired. When things are going well for us, we can become complacent or bored with our circumstances and stop acknowledging God's role in providing us with the things we possess. We may begin craving something new and exciting. It is important for us to learn how to cultivate a spiritual disposition of contentment while we are single.

The second area of study in this chapter focuses on being the bride of Christ. A bride is a woman that is preparing to be married. In our lives as Christians, we should be preparing to be with the Lord forever in eternity. It is imperative that a Christian bride not act as if a mortal husband could ever take the place of Jesus Christ in her life. There are certain things that only Christ can do for us. A Christian woman seeking to marry must not act as if her husband, Christ, is dead, seeking to marry another.

Discussion Questions

Define contentment.

_____

_____

_____

_____

_____

What do you need to be content?

_____

_____

_____

_____

_____

What is the secret of contentment?

_____

_____

_____

_____

_____

Describe a time you were discontent.

_____

_____

_____

_____

_____

What caused your discontentment? How did you get over it?

_____

_____

_____

_____

_____

How do you deal with worry?

_____

_____

_____

_____

_____

Who do you compare yourself with?

_____

_____

_____

_____

_____

What do you find yourself comparing the most?

_____

_____

_____

_____

_____

Describe a time when being bored got you into trouble.

_____

_____

_____

_____

_____

How do you keep yourself busy?

_____

_____

_____

_____

_____

What does it mean to be the bride of Christ?

_____

_____

_____

_____

_____

Relate a time when you acted as if your husband were dead.

_____

_____

_____

_____

_____

ACTIVITY:

Vow Renewal

Often when people have been married for a significant amount of time or have been through a particularly difficult patch, they will have a vow renewal or recommitment ceremony to publicly proclaim their rededication to one another. While some do this to enjoy a wedding they may not have been able to afford when they initially became husband and wife, most do it to symbolize a new beginning or to celebrate how far they've come.

At this point, you may have realized that you haven't been as faithful to your vows to God as you should have been. Or maybe you haven't fully appreciated the love that God has shown you through the years as you've walked closely beside Him. For whatever reason, you feel that you could benefit from a rededication to your first love.

For this activity, write down the vows you would profess to God at your vow renewal ceremony. Express your appreciation of what He has done. Acknowledge where you could improve in your relationship with Him and pledge to do so. State what you committed yourself to when you first obeyed the gospel, and reaffirm that you will endeavor to live up to those promises.

Every exchange of vows requires witnesses. Be sure to inform an accountability partner, elder, bible study group member, or someone else spiritually minded of your renewed commitment who will keep you accountable.

DEVOTIONAL:

I Keep Falling in Love with Him

How do we know if we are in love with God & not just going through the motions?

Our love for God should be an *active* love. God says "if you love me, keep my commandments." Christ's love should compel us to live for Him (II Cor. 5:14-15) and not just for our selfish interests and pursuits. People should be able to see our love and loyalty to God in how we love one another (John 8:31; I John 2:5, 4:20). In other words, our love should be seen as well as felt.

If we examine the characteristics associated with being in romantic love, we can develop a picture of what being in love with Jesus/God looks like.

When you are in love with a romantic partner, you put your whole heart into it. There's no such thing as spending too much time with them; in fact, you will alter your schedule to find time to spend with them. You are so excited to spend time with them you will forego things you would enjoy doing if you weren't in a relationship with them. You can't stop talking about them. It doesn't matter if your family or friends don't seem to understand your love for your partner; you will defend and protect your relationship from anyone or anything that threatens to tear you apart, including those close to you. You want to know everything about them. You take the time to learn about their interests, hobbies, and what makes them tick. Doing things that they ask of you is no hardship or burden, and you do it without complaint. You seek ways to please them and make them happy.

These are the things God wants from us. God wants us to love Him with all our heart and soul (Deut. 6:5; Matt. 22:37; Mark 12:30; Luke 10:27). He wants no one and nothing else placed above Him (Ex. 20:1-6). Christ encourages us to "take my yoke upon you and learn of me" (Matt 11:29). He wants us to leave mother and father for him (Mark 10:29). He expects us to share His love for us with other people (John 13:35). He asserts that if we love Him, we will keep His commandments (John 14:15). He calls those who are persecuted for His sake blessed (Matt 5:11; Luke 6:22).

Though God expects so much devotion from us, He gives us so much more in return. We can ask God for anything within His will, and He will give it to us (Matt 6:25; Matt. 7:11). He looks after our every need (Matt 6:25-33). He is always paying attention to us. He knows everything there is to know about us, and has known even before we were born (Jer. 1:5; Psalm 139:13). Who wouldn't want to be faithful to a love like that?

NAKED DEVOTIONAL:

Naked Power

> 5Let your conversation *be* without covetousness; and be content with such things as ye have: for he hath said, I will never leave thee, nor forsake thee. 6So that we may boldly say, The Lord is my helper, and I will not fear what man shall do unto me. Heb. 13:5-6

Naked power is power over someone or something that is unrelated to an interest in the well-being or continuation of that person or thing. In other words, the person who has the power over you isn't personally invested in the outcome of the situation; the decisions that they make have no effect on them.

In some cases, this is good. We often need a neutral third party to determine a fair way to resolve a conflict. The bible tells us if we have an issue with a brother that cannot be resolved between us to bring witnesses and eventually the church (Matt. 18:15-17).

But sometimes this can be a bad thing. Someone who has no vested interest in your well-being may use you or abuse their power over you. They may get in the way of your service to God. Paul tells the Galatians that they were running well and asks who hindered them so that they didn't obey the truth (Gal.5:7). Any person or entity that has power over you that keeps you from obeying the truth puts your salvation at risk.

God does not exert naked power over us. Over and over again in scripture we see that He cares for us and wants us to bring our burdens to

Him (I Pet5:6-7). God has proven he is interested in our well-being and wants the best for us.

If anyone or anything is preventing from obeying the Lord, get out from under its power. Don't allow yourself to be hindered or delayed from obeying the Lord because He loves you and has your best interest in mind.

Throw Rice Not Shade

This "In the Meantime" section focuses on learning how to be content for others while dealing with discontent within our personal lives. This requires that we understand that someone else's successes or failures have no bearing on what God has in store for us. Their success doesn't make ours less likely, and vice-versa. Therefore, there is no reason why we can't be happy for someone else's success. Ten strategies for being happy for others are given in this section:

1. Have fulfilling relationships
2. Fast from social media
3. Get close to other Christians
4. Stop comparing yourself and your situation to other women.
5. Stop clock watching.
6. Start praying for those entering into positions you want.
7. Get a singles' devotional.
8. Stop making marriage an idol.
9. Make your single's bucket list.
10. Work on your "list."

ACTIVITY:

Single Bucket List

"Give yourself things to look forward to and work toward instead of waiting around for marriage (*Altered,* 74)."

A bucket list is a list of things you want to accomplish before a set time. The most popular use of the bucket list is to list things you want to do before you "kick the bucket," or die. It is important to have goals that you are striving to reach, and having a timetable can motivate us to get started or to keep going forward when the going gets tough.

In this activity, create a "Single's Bucket List" for yourself of things you want to do before getting married. Below I have given you some suggested categories of activities and experiences to add to, but feel free to create your own categories as well. You can create a vision board or a video if you wish. The objective is to think critically about things you want to accomplish outside of getting married.

Books to read	Things to do	Places to go	Dreams to fulfill	Goals

ACTIVITY:

Wiping the Slate Clean

Throughout the day, our minds can get overloaded with information and images from all around us, many of which are not of God. There are many opportunities for us to compare ourselves and come up short, be overtaken with pride, or be led astray. The task to erase all of the bad programming from our minds can become overwhelming.

Have you ever noticed that to clean a black board you not only have to erase what's on it but you have to wash it? If you just wipe a blackboard, there's often chalk or ink residue left on it.

The brain is the same way. Sometimes spending a few hurried minutes with God each morning is just moving the chalk dust around and scribbling a line that will be erased and replaced by the end of the day. Not only do we have to stop sinning, we have to get the imprint of sin off our minds. We have to wipe that slate clean so that God can write something new on our hearts.

Constantly checking blogs and other social media can distract us from the things God is calling us to pay attention to. It can even have a negative effect on our mood. Maybe you stalk the social media of celebrities or your friends and come away feeling envious of their lives. You are happy when people like your statuses and upset when they don't. Following social media can be one big emotional rollercoaster.

Another source of distraction is reality TV. Shows about weddings or seeing the money and excess on the Real Housewives shows might set you down a path of discontentment. If nothing else, it causes you to spend mindless hours in front of the TV that you could be spending with God.

Instead of getting stuck in this cycle, try this: for two weeks, fast from social media of any kind—Facebook, Twitter, Instagram, Pinterest, Blogs, Celebrity sites, magazines like People and Us Weekly, Stumbled Upon, Buzz Feed, Reddit, etc.—all of it. Turn off the TV. Take yourself out of the loop for two weeks. Find something else to do with your time. You will be surprised how much time you will find in your day.

You may find you now have more time to spend with God, exercise, catch up with friends, cook, tackle your finances, or get more sleep. Instead of envying someone else's life, you get to live your own. Give God the opportunity to write some things on your heart.

When you return to social media, keep renewing your mind with the Word so that you can better decide who you want to "friend" or "follow" that can add to your life instead of breeding greed, jealousy, and other vices. You may feel the need to get rid of some people and things on your social media that aren't serving your goal serving God.

Making Yourself "Meet"

While Single & Satisfied dealt more with spiritual preparation for mate selection, "Making Yourself 'Meet'" deals with more carnal aspects of marriage preparation. The importance of mate selection being mutual is emphasized, along with the assertion that a woman should seek to be an asset instead of a liability to anyone she desires to marry. Three key areas of concern for the Christian woman seeking to marry are addressed: her reputation, her tongue, and her physical appearance.

Discussion Questions

List your assets and liabilities in relationships.

_____

_____

_____

_____

_____

_____

What type of Proverbs wife are you? How can you improve yourself in this area?

_____

_____

_____

_____

Relate the characteristics of a good name.

_____

_____

_____

_____

_____

Pick three words or phrases that describe how you want to be seen. What changes would you have to make to project this image?

_____

_____

_____

_____

_____

What behaviors do you exhibit that are contradictory to the way you want to be seen? How can you change these behaviors?

_____

_____

_____

_____

_____

Relate a time when you misrepresented yourself. Who did you misrepresent yourself to? Why? How long did you do it? Did the other person ever find out? What was the result?

_____

_____

_____

_____

_____

_____

_____

_____

_____

_____

What is your issue/problem with your tongue? How have you tried to change it? What results did this achieve?

_____

_____

_____

_____

_____

_____

Which illustration of the tongue best describes your tongue (rudder, bit, fire, fountain, etc.)? Explain.

_____

_____

_____

_____

_____

What new thing have you learned about the tongue in this section? How will it inform your conversations going forward?

_____

_____

_____

_____

_____

Think of a time you have gossiped about someone or been the subject of gossip. What caused the gossip? What effect did gossiping have on the situation/relationship?

_____

_____

_____

_____

_____

_____

How can you cultivate quietness?

_____

_____

_____

_____

_____

Name five things you like about the way you look.

_____

_____

_____

_____

_____

Name two things you don't like about the way you look.

_____

_____

Can you improve any of these things? If you can, what has stopped you from doing so?

_____

_____

_____
_____
_____

Does your style of dress show that you belong to Christ?

_____
_____
_____
_____
_____

How can you dress modestly and still be fashionable? Should you try to be fashionable at all?

_____
_____
_____
_____
_____

How do you maintain your physical body?

_____
_____
_____
_____
_____

ACTIVITY:

Setting Your Table

A key determining factor in the success of any relationship is what we as individuals bring to the table. A person can only utilize the skills at their disposal to navigate the new territory they find themselves in. It is imperative, therefore, that we begin to get a good picture of the skills and deficiencies we have so that we can improve upon them.

In this activity, we are going to examine your first relationships—those with your family. What are some common characteristics amongst your family members? What tendencies tend to repeat themselves in your family? Are these traits good or bad? Do you see any of these traits in yourself? Do others see them in you?

Family interaction is also important. What are your relationships with your family members like? Do you have relationships with them? We may be different than the members of our family, but growing up in the same or similar environments with the same style of parenting have left some similarities in our character. We may be new creatures in Christ, but in order to keep the old man from resurrecting, we have to be able to recognize his tendencies.

For this activity, draw a family tree. Who would you consider to be the roots of that tree, the most vital and largely unseen sustainers of the tree? Who forms the base? Who has branched off, staying connected but doing their own thing? Who has fallen away?

List the character traits of each group of people. Which do you share? Where do you differ? How have these traits influenced how you interact with the people that share them? Could you be in a close, intimate relationship with someone who also has these characteristics?

DEVOTIONAL:

Naked in Heels

¹¹ Put on the whole armour of God, that ye may be able to stand against the wiles of the devil...¹³ Wherefore take unto you the whole armour of God, that ye may be able to withstand in the evil day, and having done all, to stand. Ephesians 6:11,13

One of the first decisions we make every day is what we will wear. A great deal of planning and preparation goes into a great outfit. As women, we may place a significant amount of importance on our appearance. We wear certain garments to highlight our best features and hide our less attractive ones. How we dress sets the tone for the day.

In Ephesians 6, Paul stresses the importance of putting on a spiritual outfit before we go out into the world. These garments are multipurpose items that afford us protection while allowing us to fight back and defend ourselves against the Enemy. Unlike when you rush out of your house without putting your makeup on, going out without your armor in place can result in spiritual injury.

Today as you choose what you will wear and carefully attend to your hair and/or makeup, meditate on each piece of armor Paul details in Ephesians 6. How can you gird your loins with truth? What does it mean to wear the helmet of salvation? How can you best ensure that you are protected against the Enemy today? Don't leave home without your armor this day.

DEVOTIONAL:

Naked Calisthenics

23 And this I do for the gospel's sake, that I might be partaker thereof with you. 24 Know ye not that they which run in a race run all, but one receiveth the prize? So run, that ye may obtain. 25 And every man that striveth for the mastery is temperate in all things. Now they do it to obtain a corruptible crown; but we an incorruptible. 26 I therefore so run, not as uncertainly; so fight I, not as one that beateth the air: 27 But I keep under my body, and bring it into subjection: lest that by any means, when I have preached to others, I myself should be a castaway.
I Cor. 9:23-27

Exercise is very important to keeping our bodies performing well. It increases our energy level and lifts our mood. Anyone who seeks to remain healthy is encouraged to partake in physical activity at least three times a week.

Running is a particularly popular form of exercise that requires discipline and frequent practice to perfect. While many run for the health benefits, others seek to win recognition for their efforts. The accomplishment of finishing a race doesn't compare to winning the race for them. Anyone can run, but only the best runner can win the race.

Christians are encouraged to look at their journey as a race on numerous occasions in scripture. Paul reminds the Galatians that they ran well and wonders what has hindered them (Gal. 5:7). The Hebrew writer encourages us to lay aside every weight and sin and run the race set before us with patience (Heb. 12:1).

Not everyone who starts on this Christian journey will finish the race. Many will get tired and quit, be led astray, or be so weighed down by sin and the cares of this world that they cannot win the prize. Today, make sure that you are running in such a way that you can obtain your incorruptible crown. Evaluate how well you are running and what you are carrying with you along this race. Is all of it essential to winning this race? If it isn't, set it aside so that you can run better. Refocus your attention on the finish and condition yourself to be able to endure until you cross the finish line.

Submission in a Beyoncé World

Submission is a discipline that should be practiced by both Christian men and women. Both men and women are called to submit to the elders of the church, those in positions of authority, one another and the laws of the land. Wives have the additional charge to submit to their husbands.

In Ephesians 5, Paul uses the illustration of the head and the body to describe the relationships between Christ and the Church as well as between a husband and a wife. By examining the responsibilities of the head and the body within the natural world, we are better able to understand how the relationship between a husband and wife should work.

Also examined in the submission chapter was the opposite of submission—manipulation. Women may seek to manipulate men through tears, nagging, seduction, being "helpful," and false submission. It is imperative that the woman of God avoid falling back on these devices to get her way in relationships.

Discussion Questions

"It can cripple a Christian home if a woman does not value her role in being submissive to her husband." Do you agree with this statement? Explain.

_____

_____

_____

_____

_____

_____

List the characteristics of an independent woman.

_____

_____

_____

_____

_____

How can these characteristics negatively impact relationships?

_____

_____

_____

_____

_____

In what areas do you struggle with being obedient to God?

_____

_____

_____

_____

_____

How do you interpret "submit as unto the Lord?"

_____

_____

_____

_____

_____

In what ways have you sought to manipulate people?

_____

_____

_____

DEVOTIONAL:

Submission

33 And he taketh with him Peter and James and John, and began to be sore amazed, and to be very heavy; 34 And saith unto them, My soul is exceeding sorrowful unto death: tarry ye here, and watch. 35 And he went forward a little, and fell on the ground, and prayed that, if it were possible, the hour might pass from him. 36 And he said, Abba, Father, all things are possible unto thee; take away this cup from me: nevertheless not what I will, but what thou wilt. Mark 14:33-36

One of the greatest examples of submission is given to us by Jesus in the Garden of Gethsemane. At this time, Jesus knows He is about to be betrayed and handed over to die on the cross. He is feeling anguish over the task He has to complete. He'd rather not do it. Instead of being rebellious, He consults the Father and asks Him to remove the task from Him if it is the Father's will. He beseeches the Lord three times and each time ends it with an assertion that God's will be done.

When we experience difficulty submitting, whether it's to instruction and direction, a person or a situation, it is OK to experience some doubt about how you will manage to remain submissive. It's even OK to ask God to let this cup pass from you. But at the end of all of our requests, we must understand and accept that God's will is the one that will be done. This is the way that Jesus taught us to pray in the Sermon on the Mount, and this is the way that He prayed when suffering affliction Himself.

Ultimately, it is God that we are submitting to no matter the source of the directive. As long as it doesn't violate biblical or judicial law to comply, we should look at any request as if it came from the Lord. God is the one who set governments, church leadership, parents, and husbands in place. By submitting to them, we are telling Him that we are fully submitted to His will for our lives.

Reflect on this beautiful picture of submission today. Adjust your thinking so that you can acknowledge God's providence in submission instead of focusing on any inclination to rebel.

Standards Higher than Your Heels: Requirements vs. Preferences

The chapter "Standards Higher than Your Heels" deals with the expectations that a person brings to a relationship, both spoken and unspoken. It is important to realize that whether expressed or not, everyone has expectations that they expect a significant other to meet. It is important for singles to be able to distinguish between characteristics it is necessary for their mate to have and traits that are preferred but not required. All of God's requirements must be met in order for a relationship to be in accordance with His will.

Knowing what our expectations are helps us to be able to properly evaluate any prospective partners we are presented with. It is important that we also express our expectations in relationships so that the other person is aware of them and can decide if they are capable and willing to meet our expectations, and vice versa.

Discussion Questions

What's your definition of a "good man"?

_____

_____

_____

_____

_____

How have you learned what you want in a mate?

_____

_____

_____

_____

_____

How has your list of deal breakers evolved over the years? Explain.

_____

_____

_____

_____

_____

Do you have a "list"? Is it written down?

_____

_____

_____

_____

_____

Describe a time you were disappointed because you didn't properly communicate your expectations. How could you have better expressed what you wanted?

_____

_____

_____

_____

_____

Explain the difference between a requirement and a preference. How do you determine if something is a requirement?

_____

_____

_____

_____

_____

_____

Are you ready to be married? Explain.

_____

_____

_____

_____

ACTIVITY:

The List

In this activity, create your "list." Divide the characteristics that you look for in a mate between two categories: Requirements and preferences. For each requirement, give an explanation for why you have made it a requirement.

Requirements	**Preferences**

ACTIVITY:

Your Real List

Many women struggle with trying to create a list of desirable characteristics that they want in a mate. They worry about whether or not the things that they place on their list are too superficial or unimportant. They wonder if God even cares about their preferences. Sometimes they think they know what they want, but when they get into a relationship with their "ideal mate," they discover that they want something different. This can discourage many women.

Instead of being overly critical of your list, use this technique I learned from Dr. Gerri Tartt for identifying what you really want in a mate. Concentrate on a non-romantic relationship in your life that works well. Isolate the characteristics the other person possesses that make a loving relationship with them possible. What do you need to have a good relationship with someone?

Now, take it further. Take the characteristics you have listed and state what this reveals to you about what you require in a loving relationship. Does the fact that you appreciate how your mother never misses your special events mean that you value someone who is dependable? Investigate your reasons to discover what it is that makes a relationship with you successful, and then translate that into your "real" list of qualities you want in a prospective mate.

ACTIVITY:

Relationship Résumé

A résumé is a document that is sent out to potential employers to show them how suitable of a candidate you are for a position with their company. It contains all of your pertinent information, including your education, skills, previous experience, and even your objectives for your career. You want your résumé to clearly state your strengths and the unique skills you can bring to the job. A résumé helps employers decide who is the most qualified for a position.

For this activity, fill out a "relationship résumé." List your objectives (to be a wife, etc.), relationship education, awards, previous "jobs" and your responsibilities at each job, and any marketable relationship skills you have that you think a man looking for a wife would be interested in.

ACTIVITY:

Want Ads

Create a relationship job listing. Express what type of employer you are and what type of employee you are seeking. List your requirements and preferences as to experience and skills. Be sure to include what you have to offer in your listing as well.

Ex. Spirit-led Christian woman seeks God-fearing leader to marry. All applicants must have a personal relationship with the Lord, great communication skills, and at least 18 years' experience treating their mother with respect and care. A man with a good sense of humor is preferred. Starting salary is a daily dose of love, home-cooked meals, and a clean home with bonus eligibility.

_____

_____

_____

_____

_____

_____

_____

_____

_____

"Meet" Mates/Digging Deeper

"Meet Mates" explores the issue of soul mates, concluding that God chose what we marry, not whom we marry. God decided that a man should marry a woman, but allows us to exercise our free will in choosing our marriage partner.

While God does not choose our marriage partner, He has provided us with biblical principles that we can use in our mate selection process. It wouldn't be a good idea to base our decision on our feelings. It is evident in how much the world's views on what makes someone marriage material changes that we cannot base our opinions on their standards, either.

Three important principles of mate selection that can be gleaned from biblical example are explored:

1. Choose a partner with the same religious convictions.
2. Involve God in the mate selection process.
3. Involve elders in the mate selection process.

In "Digging Deeper," we examined these areas in further detail, discovering what it truly means to be unequally yoked, learning the basics of prayer and confirmation, and defining the sort of elders that should be involved in your mate selection process.

The topic of impatience and trying to hurry God's timetable was also introduced in a discussion of Ishmael. Ishmael was representative of Sarai's inability to trust in God to keep His word, looking at her circumstances, and trying to use logic to "decipher" God's plan.

Discussion Questions

How have America's views on marriage changed in your lifetime?

_____

_____

_____

_____

_____

How important is it to be "equally yoked"?

_____

_____

_____

_____

_____

Describe a time you have been unequally yoked with someone. This can be in a relationship, friendship, working on a project, with a roommate, etc.

_____

_____

_____

_____

_____

_____

Properly Defined: Provide your definition of the following terms. Explain.

Headship

_____

_____

_____

_____

_____

Submission

_____

_____

_____

_____

_____

Respect

_____

_____

_____

_____

_____

Love

_____

_____

_____

_____

_____

Provision

_____

_____

_____

_____

_____

Leading

_____

_____

_____

_____

_____

Forgiveness

_____

_____

_____

_____

_____

Unfaithfulness

_____

_____

_____

_____

_____

Communication

_____

_____

_____

_____

_____

What do you pray for? How do you pray? When?

_____

_____

_____

_____

_____

_____

Describe a time you prayed and the confirmation you received that your prayer had been answered.

_____

_____

_____

_____

_____

Explain why it's important to have elders involved in the selection process.

_____

_____

_____

_____

_____

Discuss a time when being impatient led you to make the wrong decision. Did your reason for doing it match Sarai's reasons? What were the results? How could you have reacted differently?

_____

_____

_____

Altered before the Altar

ACTIVITY:

Pray Until Something Happens

(P.U.S.H.)

When I was at Purdue University, every Saturday the ladies who went to the Christian Student Center would hold a ladies' prayer breakfast. We had a big poster board where we wrote our names, the date and our prayer requests before sharing them aloud and praying for each other.

Each week we would read over the things we had written the previous weeks and cross any prayers that were answered off the list. Then we would share our testimony with one another. It was amazing to have a visual representation of how God was working in all of our lives. Nothing felt as good as seeing a woman cross something off of her list that she'd been praying about for a long time. It helped us to focus on how God answers our prayers and helped us realize when He had answered us.

I know for me, when I pay attention to my prayer life, I see how things that I've prayed for have been resolved in ways that could only be God. I think we all need to be able to see the hand of God moving in our lives, to know that He is listening to us as we are listening to Him and trying to live obedient to His word.

To that end, I want you to begin keeping a prayer journal detailing what you pray about each day. Write the date above each new prayer request. When you have identified an answer to that prayer, write the date next to it and record how you knew it was God answering your prayer. It is my hope that by being mindful of what you are praying for, you will begin looking and listening for the answers and not missing the subtle ways in which God is trying to lead and direct you.

ACTIVITY:

Assemble Your Council

I believe that every young woman needs to be taught of an older woman as Paul exhorts in Titus 2. The Bible gives the qualifications of these older women as well as what they are to teach the younger women.

Read Titus 2:3-5 and think about the things enumerated there. List the ways that you excel and the ways in which you are deficient in each area. Create a list of older Christian women you admire for the way they excel in areas in which you are deficient. Evaluate how well they fit the qualities that Titus outlines for an older woman to possess. Pick an older woman (or a few) to become an apprentice to.

An apprentice is someone who is taught a skill or trade by a master in the field, usually one on one. It is more than mentorship—it is teaching someone everything you know about the subject. The person that you choose to guide your apprenticeship has to be someone that you have no problem telling anything you're feeling, someone you will listen to and heed their advice.

Go to God and pray about the women on your list. Ask Him to show you the woman He would have you to ask to teach you how to be a great woman of God. Find a creative way to ask her to teach you. You can make a card, take her out to lunch, or bake a batch of cookies for her. If the woman you have selected is not able to accept, don't stop looking. God will provide you with someone to fulfill the desire and need that you have.

DEVOTIONAL:

Unequally Yoked

14 Be ye not unequally yoked together with unbelievers: for what fellowship hath righteousness with unrighteousness? and what communion hath light with darkness? II Cor. 6:14

When we think about being unequally yoked with someone, our minds may immediately go to a romantic partner. More specifically, the emphasis seems to be placed on not marrying someone who is not a Christian. Yet in this passage, Paul is not speaking of marriage at all. He is talking about the associations that the Corinthians had with unbelievers and how they hadn't separated themselves from them. This applies to marriage, of course, but it goes beyond marriage into every part of our lives.

Paul exhorts the Corinthian people to come out from among unbelievers and be separate. Some of the believers had accepted God's love but hadn't altered their associations and practices accordingly. Paul uses himself and the disciples as an example to show the people how to behave. He emphasized how their conduct left no room for anyone to condemn God, nor did it place a stumbling block before anyone.

You can be unequally yoked with someone in the church just like you can be with someone outside of the church. We are called to be a peculiar people, set apart to serve God. We cannot afford to let half-hearted believers and their slothfulness toward the things of God influence us anymore than we can let someone entrenched in sin influence us. Shake any yoke that pulls you off the path of salvation.

DEVOTIONAL:

Praying in Bitterness of Soul

9 So Hannah rose up after they had eaten in Shiloh, and after they had drunk. Now Eli the priest sat upon a seat by a post of the temple of the LORD. 10 And she was in bitterness of soul, and prayed unto the LORD, and wept sore. 11 And she vowed a vow, and said, O LORD of hosts, if thou wilt indeed look on the affliction of thine handmaid, and remember me, and not forget thine handmaid, but wilt give unto thine handmaid a man child, then I will give him unto the LORD all the days of his life, and there shall no razor come upon his head. 12 And it came to pass, as she continued praying before the LORD, that Eli marked her mouth. 13 Now Hannah, she spake in her heart; only her lips moved, but her voice was not heard: therefore Eli thought she had been drunken. 14 And Eli said unto her, How long wilt thou be drunken? put away thy wine from thee. 15 And Hannah answered and said, No, my lord, I am a woman of a sorrowful spirit: I have drunk neither wine nor strong drink, but have poured out my soul before the LORD. 16 Count not thine handmaid for a daughter of Belial: for out of the abundance of my complaint and grief have I spoken hitherto. I Sam. 1:9-16

The biblical account of Hannah's prayer is illustrative of a woman deep in anguish who turns to the Lord for help. Hannah is barren, and her husband's other wife torments her about it. She finds herself so overcome with feelings of sorrow which she prays fervently for God to requite with a child of her own. She doesn't speak aloud, but she's praying so hard that her lips are moving as if she's drunk. This is a woman pouring her heart out to God.

What strikes me about Hannah, and about David and others in the bible who petitioned the Lord with strong emotion and conviction, is not the strength of her emotion, but what she does after she pours out her request to the Lord. After Hannah prays, she leaves and returns to her family. She eats and drinks and her countenance is no longer sad. Once Hannah gave her cares over to the Lord, she trusted in His answer and went on as if her request had been granted.

Sometimes when we pray, we may feel the urge to continue to turn a problem over in our head or worry about the outcome. Sometimes we can't seem to stop ourselves from frowning or crying over the very thing we have just entreated God for. But the biblical example in Hannah's case and others is that once we take a care to the Lord, no matter how burdensome, we leave it there.

Today, stop trying to pick up the things you left at the feet of the Lord in prayer. Go on about your life as if you have already received His answer concerning your situation. Stop standing around waiting to see if God is going to do anything in the timeframe you want Him to do things in. God will work things together for good for those who love Him and are called according to His purpose (Rom. 8:28) without your supervision and suggestions. Trust God with your problems, or don't give them to Him. Accept the rest that God wants to give you and lay that heavy burden at His feet.

Call Him Ishmael

An "Ishmael" is a man that you seek out trying to circumvent God's timing in your romantic life. In the biblical account of Ishmael, Abram's son with Hagar, we see that Ishmael and Isaac share some similarities, but only one of them is an heir to the promise God made to Abram.

If you are unsure whether or not a man might be an Ishmael, here are a few characteristics that may identify one to you:

1. He will be a wild man.
2. He will be against everyone and everyone will be against him.
3. He will live in hostility toward all his brothers.
4. He will have many nations.

It is important to remember that Ishmael was Sarai's idea. Even though she came to regret it, it was Sarai who encouraged Abram to sleep with her handmaid so that they could have a child. The lesson to be learned from this story is to trust God and His timing no matter what the situation may look like to us.

ACTIVITY:

Almost Doesn't Count

When it comes to mate selection, most women can express what they believe their ideal man is like. Yet a large number of women still fall into relationships with men who are clearly not suitable matches. It's almost as if they give up on finding Mr. Right and settle for Mr. Almost-But-Not-Quite-Right.

Many women seek out "Ishmaels" when they grow impatient with God's timing in their lives. They will settle for a man who appears to have it together or that logic dictates is a good choice in the absence of a clear conscience about him.

I am a firm believer in the idea that knowing what you are susceptible to gives you a better chance of protecting yourself against it. It's important to know both the type of man you are looking for and the type of man the devil may send your way that causes you to settle. So in this activity, we are going to explore your Ishmael.

All of our "Ishmaels" look different. We are willing to compromise in different areas and tolerate different things. Describe your Ishmael. What does he look like? What characteristics does your "almost-but-not-quite-right-for-you man" possess? What sort of man do you seek out or think about when you are feeling lonely, impatient or frustrated?

Now describe your Isaac. What makes him different from an Ishmael? What makes him an Isaac? What makes him someone you should wait for?

_____

_____

_____

_____

_____

_____

_____

_____

_____

_____

_____

_____

_____

_____

_____

_____

_____

_____

_____

_____

_____

_____

_____

_____

_____

_____

_____

_____

_____

_____

_____

_____

_____

Maintaining the Proper Relationship with the Opposite Sex

The key to maintaining the proper relationship with the opposite sex is to understand the importance of our thoughts, actions, and appearance. Our relationships with members of the opposite sex should be friendly, familial and holy. We should also be accountable when engaging in relationships as we are representatives of Christ.

When evaluating a perspective mate, it is important to set boundaries, meet in environments conducive to getting to know someone, and look for red flags that alert you to deal-breakers.

Discussion Questions

What is a good age for you to start pursuing a romantic relationship? Explain.

_____

_____

_____

_____

_____

Identify 3 dating behaviors you would like to emulate.

_____

_____

_____

Identify 3 dating behaviors you would like to avoid.

_____

_____

_____

Name 3 ways you should think of men.

_____

_____

_____

Why is how a situation appears important?

_____

_____

_____

List ways you can avoid the appearance of evil.

_____

_____

_____

_____

What have your actions said about how you view men?

_____

_____

_____

_____

List some things you would consider to be a red flag.

_____

_____

_____

_____

_____

List things you would do/places you would go on a date.

_____

_____

_____

_____

_____

How would going to those places or participating in those activities aid you in getting to know someone?

_____

_____

_____

_____

_____

List ways you can keep God involved in the process.

_____

_____

_____

_____

_____

Getting it In: Fornication, Shacking up and Body Politics

Sexual sin isn't any worse than any other sin, but it is one of the only sins you commit against your own body. While some Christians may seek to downplay sexual sin, God has not changed His stance regarding fornication and adultery. As Christians, our bodies are not our own and we do what we want with them. Christ purchased the church with His blood, and as members of His church, we belong to Him in both body and spirit.

Sex may be influenced by body chemistry and hormones, but it is more than just a biological urge. It is what sets the marital relationship apart from all others as well as being the vehicle through which God brings forth life. We should enjoy sex within the bounds of the relationship that God established for us to enjoy it in--marriage. We must not let our hunger cause us to stumble.

Even if you aren't committing fornication, cohabitating with someone gives sin an opportunity. Moreover, it hints at sexual immorality in a way that may cause others to stumble.

Discussion Questions

How is sexual sin different from other sins?

_____

_____

_____

_____

_____

How does body chemistry play into sexual attraction?

_____

_____

_____

_____

_____

True or false: If you commit fornication with someone, you have to marry them. Explain.

_____

_____

_____

_____

_____

How are fornicators like Esau?

_____

_____

_____

_____

_____

What does it mean to build an altar to someone?

_____

_____

_____

_____

_____

Why is cohabitating (shacking up) wrong?

_____

_____

_____

_____

_____

DEVOTIONAL:

In the Flesh

12Let not sin therefore reign in your mortal body, that ye should obey it in the lusts thereof...16Know ye not, that to whom ye yield yourselves as servants to obey, his servants ye are to whom ye obey; whether of sin unto death, or of obedience unto righteousness? Romans 6:12, 16

Paul is constantly exhorted the believers of his day not to let sin rule over them like a monarch that they are required to obey. He doesn't say this from a position of superiority, looking down on others and wondering why they can't get themselves together and live right, but from a place of humbleness and humility, knowing that God has delivered him. He knows what it's like to want to do good, but have evil present with him (Rom. 7:21).

There are things that we really want to do, but our carnal side sometimes holds us back from accomplishing them. While for some this is their physical lust for another person, for others it's a much sneakier thing. Overindulgence in food, laziness, talking too much, gossiping, shopping excessively, not being able to control angry impulses, pride, arrogance, jealousy, addiction—any sin that makes it impossible for you to do the good things you want to do or achieve your purpose/calling is ruling over you. While you may seek to justify your weaknesses, the truth of the matter is, at the end of all the excuses we find ourselves. At the end of all inner struggle is the fight to make our flesh obey our spirit.

Today think about the things you find yourself repeatedly struggling with. Concentrate on what is keeping you from being able to grow in your life. Then meditate on the fact that God broke the bonds of sin. Read Psalms 107 and think about all of the times and all of the ways in which God has rescued His people. Know that what you are struggling with is not too big for God.

Achan for Forgiveness

The final chapter of *Altered before the Altar* is about forgiveness. The way that God has provided for us to be forgiven of sin after we have obeyed the gospel and been baptized for the remission of our sins is through repentance and confession. Repentance is a recognition that you have trespassed against God that leads to a godly sorrow. It is a turning away from sin. Confession is admitting your sin and seeking forgiveness.

Discussion Questions

What are the characteristics of repentance?

_____

_____

_____

_____

_____

How does one confess their sin?

_____

_____

_____

_____

_____

Explain how our forgiveness is tied to our forgiveness of others.

_____

_____

_____

_____

_____

DEVOTIONAL:

Naked Branches

3 He healeth the broken in heart, and bindeth up their wounds. Psalms 147:3

I love the fall. There's just something about leaves changing colors and the crispness in the air that makes me feel alive. Like most people, though, I don't care too much for the sight of all those trees when they lose their leaves. The same leaves I love to see change shrivel up and die, and the tree just lets them fall away. It's not a pretty process, but it is a necessary one.

Similarly, forgiveness is a process that isn't attractive, but one we must complete. It is the only instance in which set the standard that we are measured against. God forgives us in the same measure that we forgive others. Many who struggle with an unwillingness to forgive don't realize that God isn't going to forgive them of their sins as long as they hold on to their hurt feelings and the wrong done to them.

People do awful things to one other, some out of ignorance and others intentionally. Some things done to you may have left you deeply scarred and feeling unable to trust or feel safe. Yet God still call us to forgive and continue to extend ourselves to others.

It may seem as if God is asking too much of you when He calls you to forgive, but God wouldn't put more on you than you could bear (I Cor. 10:13). Moreover, God can heal any wounds you have if you would just turn your cares over to Him.

Holding on to hurt and pain is like a tree trying to hold on to a bunch of dead leaves. The leaves no longer have any life in them. Once you shed those leaves and rest, you give God a chance to heal you. In His time, you will bloom again. Your leaves will have life and purpose. You won't be feeding something dead anymore.

About the Author

Erica Denise Hearns first began writing at the age of five with a story about a princess named Jasmine (which she insists was NOT based on the Disney fairytale). She was first published at the age of eight and has won numerous creative writing and oratory awards. She has published several poems and essays and even authored an advice column for the newsletter for the Horizons-Upward Bound program. She graduated with a B.A. in English from the University of Central Florida in 2008.

Erica was inspired to write *Altered before the Altar* when she realized that the teenage and young adult women she taught needed some help putting dating, love and relationships into the proper perspective—and so did she. *Altered before the Altar* is Erica's first published book.

www.ingramcontent.com/pod-product-compliance
Lightning Source LLC
Chambersburg PA
CBHW071832020426
42331CB00007B/1693